Editor
Eric Migliaccio

Editor in Chief
Ina Massler Levin, M.A.

Creative Director
Karen J. Goldfluss, M.S. Ed.

Cover Artist
Barb Lorseyedi

Illustrator
Mark Mason

Art Coordinator
Renée Mc Elwee

Imaging
Rosa C. See

Publisher
Mary D. Smith, M.S. Ed.

The classroom teacher may reproduce copies of the materials in this book for use in a single classroom only. The reproduction of any part of the book for other classrooms or for an entire school or school system is strictly prohibited. No part of this publication may be transmitted, stored, or recorded in any form without written permission from the publisher.

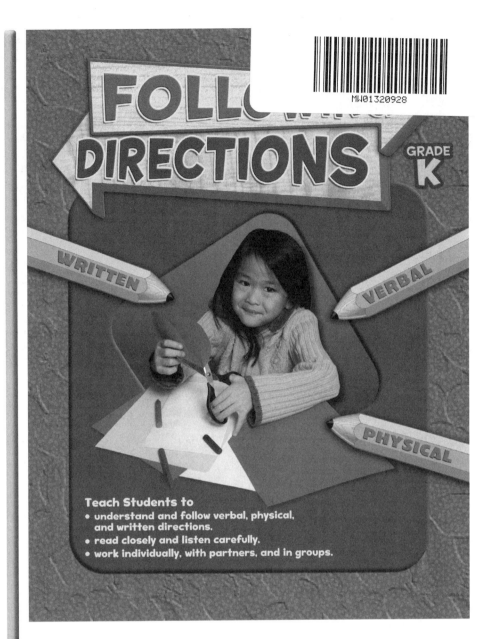

Author
Susan Mackey Collins, M. Ed.

Teacher Created Resources
6421 Industry Way
Westminster, CA 92683
www.teachercreated.com

ISBN: 978-1-4206-8710-1

© *2012 Teacher Created Resources*
Made in U.S.A.

Table of Contents

Introduction 3
Meeting Standards 4
Verbal and Physical
    Red, Yellow, and Blue 5
    Our Class Is Going on a Trip 6
    Getting the Class in Shape 7
    Making a Human Bar Graph 8
    Following Directions with Ordinal Numbers 12
    Stop! That's Not Correct. 14
    Follow the Pointing Arrow 16
    Acting Out Every Emotion 18
    Move Along with Each Direction 19
    Walk Across the Capitals 20
    Doing the Duct Walk 22
Writing and Written
    Find the One That Is Different 23
    What's Before, Between, and After? 24
    One Really Hot Dot-to-Dot 25
    An Alphabet Connect the Dots 26
    Have Some First-Letter Fun 27
    Should You Circle or Underline? 28
    Red Triangles and Blue Squares 29
    How Many Do You See? 30
    Shape Names and Numbers 31
    Same Beginning Sound 32
    Ending With the Same Sound 33
    Write Lowercase Letters 34
    Match the Letter to the Sound 35
    Trace Before You Write 36
    More Trace Before You Write 37
    Color By the Numbers 38
    Trace All of the Shapes 39
    Writing and Drawing Nouns 40
    Listen and Then Write 41
Partners and Groups
    How Words Begin and End 42
    Getting to Know Each Other 46
Answer Key 47

Introduction

All students need to be able to successfully follow directions. The ability to follow directions is a lifelong skill that must be practiced and continuously developed. Learning this skill can help a child be successful not only in his or her academics, but also in the time he or she spends outside of the learning environment of school. Learning the skills required to follow directions is essential to success in all areas of life.

Why is it important to place such an emphasis on the skills needed to follow directions? Because directions truly are everywhere, they are a part of daily life. Playing a game, reading a map, putting together a toy, cooking a recipe, completing an assignment—all require the ability to correctly follow directions. Students who are skilled at following directions most often have also mastered the art of listening. Listening skills are a key element in following directions. Students must pay attention to details in directions with both written and oral information.

Following Directions: Grade K is written to help facilitate and increase a student's ability to better focus on and follow different types of directions in a variety of academic areas. This book is an invaluable resource that is divided into three main sections:

- **Verbal and Physical Directions**
- **Writing and Written Directions**
- **Partners and Groups**

Each section of this book stresses the importance of developing the skills needed to follow directions accurately. The worksheets and activities in the book guide the students through various levels of performance as well as the key elements of following directions.

The worksheets and activities in *Following Directions: Grade K* can be completed in any order. A teacher or parent can start working at the beginning of the book and work through to the end of the book, or he or she can choose to skip through the activities and complete different pages in the various sections. No matter which order is used, the skills gained from the lessons in this book will be a great asset to any student.

Now there is nothing left to do but get started, and that's a direction that is fun and easy to follow!

Meeting Standards

Each lesson in *Following Directions: Grade K* meets one or more of the following standards, which are used with permission from McREL.

Copyright 2010, McREL, Mid-continent Research for Education and Learning.
Address: 4601 DTC Boulevard, Suite 500, Denver, CO 80237.
Telephone: 303-337-0990. Website: *www.mcrel.org/standards-benchmarks.*

Note: To align McREL standards to the Common Core Standards, go to *www.mcrel.org.*

Standards and Benchmarks	Page #
Demonstrates perseverance	
❖ Concentrates mental and physical energies to meet the demands of the task	5–11, 14–20, 23, 25–26, 38, 41–46
Understands and applies basic and advanced properties of the concepts of numbers	
❖ Counts whole numbers (i.e., both cardinal and ordinal numbers)	12–13, 36–37
❖ Understands symbolic, concrete, and pictorial representations of numbers (e.g., written numerals, objects in sets, number lines)	31
Uses grammatical and mechanical conventions in written composition	
❖ Uses conventions of printing in writing (e.g., forms letters in print, uses upper and lowercase letters of the alphabet, spaces between words and sentences, writes left-to-right and top-to-bottom, includes margins)	34
❖ Uses nouns in written compositions (e.g., singular, plural, possessive)	40
Uses the general skills and strategies of the reading process	
❖ Understands how print is organized and read (e.g. identifies front and back covers, title page, author, and illustrator; follows words from left-right and from top-to-bottom; knows the significance of the spaces between words; knows the difference between letters, words, and sentences; understands the use of capitalization and punctuation as text boundaries)	21–22, 24, 27–28, 30, 32–33
❖ Uses basic elements of phonetic analysis (e.g., common letter/sound relationships, beginning and ending consonants, spelling patterns, contractions) to decode unknown words.	35
Understands and applies basic and advanced properties of the concepts of measurement	
❖ Understands basic properties of (e.g., number of sides, corners, square corners) and similarities and differences between simple geometric shapes	29, 39

Student Directions   *Verbal and Physical*

Red, Yellow, and Blue

Materials Needed: three crayons (one blue, one red, one yellow)

Directions: Place the three crayons on your desk. Listen to your teacher read each direction written below. Follow each direction.

1. Stand up beside your desk.
2. Put one hand under your desk.
3. Pick up the blue crayon with your right hand.
4. Move the blue crayon to your left hand.
5. Pick up the yellow crayon with your right hand.
6. Place the yellow and blue crayons on the desktop.
7. Sit down.
8. Place the red crayon between the yellow and blue crayon.
9. Clap three times.
10. Use the red crayon to write your first name: _____

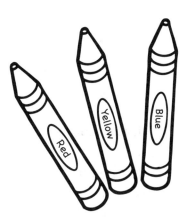

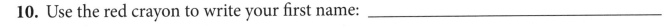

Something Extra: In the space below, draw a picture. Color the picture with only the blue, red, and yellow crayons.

Teacher Directions *Verbal and Physical*

Our Class Is Going on a Trip

Directions: Use the letters of the alphabet to play "Our Class Is Going on a Trip."

- Choose a student to begin. Choose a letter. Write the letter on the board where the students can see the letter. Cross off the letter on this worksheet once the letter has been used.

A	B	C	D	E	F	G	H	I
J	K	L	M	N	O	P	Q	R
S	T	U	V	W	X	Y	Z	

- Tell the student to repeat after you: "Our class is going on a trip, and we will take a/an _____." The student will fill in the blank with a word that starts with the letter the teacher has given the student. For example, if the student has been given the letter "C," he might say, "Our class is going on a trip, and we will take a <u>camera</u>." If the class agrees the word the student says starts with the letter you have given, then you should write the word on the board. You should say the starting letter, and the class should repeat the letter. You should then say the word, and the class should repeat the word.

- At this point, choose another letter and another student. You do not have to use all of the letters during this activity; however, it is a good idea to let each child have a turn deciding what to take on the class trip.

- If a student cannot think of a word that starts with the letter that is given, the student can ask a classmate for help. Or, instead, you can help the student find a word by giving him two or three word choices. For example, if the letter given is "s" and the student is unable to think of a word, you can say, "Snail, cup, or brownie." The student can then choose from the words given.

Options

- The class trip might be to a specific place, and so the items needed must all relate to the place the class is going.
- You might make it a rule that all answers be funny or silly.
- For an extra challenge, the students might be asked to repeat the word that was said before their turn and then add their own word. For example, they would say, "Our class is going on a trip and we will take a map and a picnic."

Teacher Directions *Verbal and Physical*

Getting the Class in Shape

Directions: For this activity the students will need space to move. As a group, they will be using their bodies to create shapes.

- Divide the class into two groups. The groups do not have to be equal; however, each member of the group must participate each time.
- Read the name of a shape or number from the list below. Read the name slowly and clearly. Remind the students to listen carefully as you read a direction.
- Tell the students in each group that they need to use their bodies to create the shape or shape of the number as quickly as possible. The group to create the shape or number shape first is the winner for that turn. Give the students an example before play begins. Use the drawing below to help you. Remind students that if a number is given, they must create the number shape and not just represent the number. In other words, two students standing side by side is not the number 2.

Example: triangle

List of Shapes and Numbers

circle	arrow	ten
square	heart	one
rectangle	diamond	four
line	seven	eleven

Teacher Directions *Verbal and Physical*

Making a Human Bar Graph

Materials Needed: scissors; cards on pages 9–11; masking tape (optional)

Directions: Use the cards on the next two pages to help students create human bar graphs. Cut the cards apart from the directions. The cards will be used to help students understand the concepts of more and less and also the importance of following directions as they physically create each bar graph.

First, find an area where students have space to make several lines. Students will remain in their seats until a direction calls for them to move and stand. Next, decide on a set of bar graph cards to use from pages 9, 10, and 11. Place the cards on the floor in a horizontal row leaving about 12 inches between each card. (If desired, use masking tape to help create the lines where the cards are placed for the graphs if needed as an extra visual for the students.) The cards should be shown to the students before they are placed on the floor so the students know each choice. Students are able to get out of their seats if they need to see the cards again.

Read the questions that go with each set of cards slowly and clearly to the students. Remind the students to listen carefully as you read each set of directions. Once a student hears the correct direction, he or she will line up behind the correct picture/word card. When each set is complete, the students should be able to tell which items have more and which items have less.

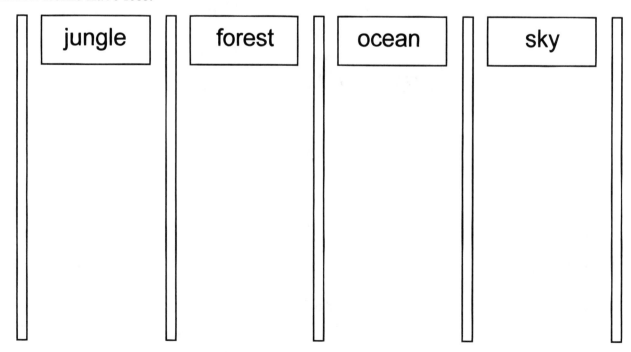

#8710 Following Directions — 8 — ©Teacher Created Resources

Teacher Directions   Verbal and Physical

Making a Human Bar Graph (cont.)

Questions for Set 1 Cards:

1. Do you like proteins such as beans, pork chops, and steak better than grains, fruits, or dairy foods? Line up behind the protein card.

2. Do you like grains such as breads, pasta, and tortillas better than fruits, dairy, or proteins? Like up behind the grains card.

3. Do you like dairy foods such as cheese, milk, and yogurt better than grains, fruits, or proteins? Line up behind the dairy card.

4. Do you like fruits such as strawberries, peaches, and bananas better than dairy foods, grains, or meats? Line up behind the fruits card.

Teacher Directions **Verbal and Physical**

Making a Human Bar Graph *(cont.)*

Questions for Set 2 Cards:

1. Do you ride a bus to get home from school? Line up behind the bus card.
2. Do you ride a car to get home from school? Line up behind the car card.
3. Do you ride a bicycle to get home from school? Line up behind the bicycle card.
4. Do you walk to get home from school? Line up behind the walker card.

Teacher Directions **Verbal and Physical**

Making a Human Bar Graph (cont.)

Questions for Set 3 Cards:

1. Do you like summer better than spring, winter, or fall? Line up behind "Summer."
2. Do you like fall better than spring, winter, or summer? Line up behind "Fall."
3. Do you like winter better than summer, spring, or fall? Line up behind "Winter."
4. Do you like spring better than summer, fall, or winter? Line up behind "Spring."

Teacher Directions — *Verbal and Physical*

Following Directions with Ordinal Numbers

Materials Needed: copies of page 13 (one per student)

Directions: Explain to the students that ordinal numbers are words like *first, second, third,* and *fourth.* Tell the students you will be giving directions out loud that involve ordinal numbers.

Before beginning the activity, have each student complete page 13. Each student should then have six cards on his or her desk: one red, one blue, one yellow, one green, one purple, and one orange.

Once the students have completed page 13, read the numbered directions below to the class. Be sure to read all the directions below slowly and clearly. Walk around the room and monitor each student's movements after a direction is read to be sure he or she understands each direction.

Directions

1. Place the colored cards in a line on your desk. It does not matter which color you start the line with.
2. If the red square is not already first, move the red square so that it is first in the line.
3. Move the green square so that it is third in line.
4. Move the orange square so that it is sixth in line.
5. Move the blue square so that it is second in line.
6. Move the purple square so that it is fifth in line.
7. Move the yellow square so that it is fourth in line.
8. Look at your line of squares. See if they are in this correct order:

First	Second	Third	Fourth	Fifth	Sixth
red	blue	green	yellow	purple	orange

Student Directions — **Verbal and Physical**

Following Directions with Ordinal Numbers (cont.)

Materials Needed: scissors, crayons (red, blue, yellow, green, purple, orange)

Directions: Read the color name on each card. Color each card that color. Cut out each square.

red	blue
yellow	green
purple	orange

Teacher Directions **Verbal and Physical**

Stop! That's Not Correct

Materials Needed: copies of page 15 (one per student); red crayons (one per student); one roll of masking tape; craft sticks or rulers (one per student)

Directions: Read the lists below out loud and in any order to the students. The lists are not in the correct order or sequence. When students hear the list is no longer in sequence, they will hold up their stop signs (from page 15) to show they have heard a problem with the order of the list. You can also let the students say the word "stop" as they hold up their signs. At that point, call on a student who has held up a stop sign and ask for him or her to tell what the correct order should be. Students will then put down their stop signs, and you can begin reading again from a new list.

Hint: If no students hear how the list is out of sequence, write the list on the board and then read the list again to help the students find a way to put the list in the correct order.

List #1	1 • 2 • 3 • 4 • 5 • 8 • 9 • 10
List #2	Sunday • Monday • Tuesday • Thursday • Wednesday • Friday • Saturday
List #3	21 • 22 • 23 • 27 • 24 • 25 • 26
List #4	January • February • April • March • May • June
List #5	A • B • C • D • F • E • G • H • I
List #6	10 • 9 • 8 • 7 • 6 • 4 • 5 • 3 • 2 • 1
List #7	July • August • September • November • October • December
List #8	Q • R • S • U • T • V
List #9	11 • 12 • 13 • 14 • 15 • 17 • 16 • 18 • 19 • 20
List #10	ant • bear • cat • dog • fish • elephant • giraffe

Student Directions *Verbal and Physical*

Stop! That's Not Correct

Directions: Color the stop sign red. Cut out the stop sign. With your teacher's help, tape the sign to a ruler or craft stick.

Teacher Directions   *Verbal and Physical*

Follow the Pointing Arrow

Materials Needed: copies of page 17 (one per student); yellow crayons (one per student); scissors (one pair per student)

Directions: Help your students learn directions and following directions by completing the following activity.

Students will use the arrow from page 17 to show they understand each direction given by the teacher. Use the list below to help instruct the students on each direction. Be sure to visually check the class after each direction is completed to see that each student has a correct understanding of the direction.

Explain to the class they will use their arrow to complete each action. Be sure to read slowly and clearly.

Have students stand beside their desks before beginning the activity and have their arrows in their hands.

Direction #1:	Point the arrow to the right.
Direction #2:	Point the arrow up.
Direction #3:	Point the arrow to the left.
Direction #4:	Point the arrow down.
Direction #5:	Point the arrow at the classroom clock.
Direction #6:	Point the arrow at someone beside you.
Direction #7:	Point the arrow to the front of the class.
Direction #8:	Point the arrow to the back of the class.
Direction #9:	Point the arrow up high.
Direction #10:	Point the arrow down low.
Direction #11:	Point the arrow at yourself.
Direction #12:	Point the arrow at your teacher.
Direction #13:	Put the arrow under your desk.
Direction #14:	Put the arrow on your desk.

Student Directions *Verbal and Physical*

Follow the Pointing Arrow

Directions: Color the arrow yellow. Cut out the arrow.

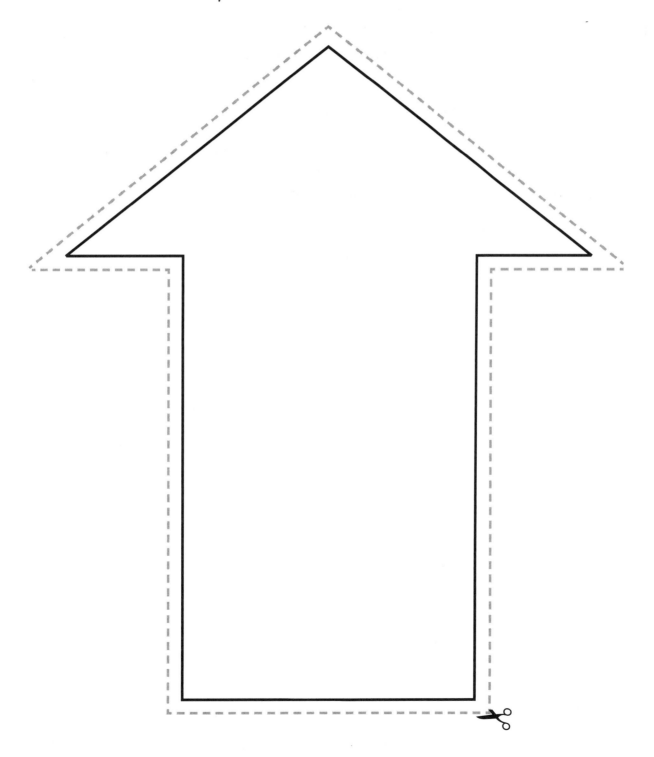

Teacher Directions *Verbal and Physical*

Acting Out Every Emotion

Directions: Tell each student to stand beside his or her desk. Tell the students you are going to do an activity about emotions and following directions. Ask any of the students if they know what emotions are. After the class has provided a satisfactory definition, explain that people's facial expressions and body language often give us a clue to which emotion a person is feeling.

Tell the class you will read out a word that is an emotion or feeling. The students are to use facial expression to pantomime the word or emotion. Check each student's expression to see that he or she understands the word. Be sure to let students look at each other's expressions and once the students have their expressions, be sure to add in one of your own. Have fun creating the best emotional face you can!

The list below can be used in any order.

Show me a _____ face!

- sad
- brave
- serious
- happy
- shy
- scared
- surprised

- afraid
- nervous
- dreamy
- shocked
- amazed
- furious
- cheerful

Teacher Directions **Verbal and Physical**

Move Along with Each Direction

Directions: Have students stand beside their desks. Use the list of motions to see how well students listen and follow directions. Watch carefully to see that each student performs each move correctly. Be sure to read each direction slowly and clearly.

1. Stand and balance on one foot.
2. Stand and balance on the opposite foot.
3. Hop in place on both feet.
4. Sit down.
5. Put your head on your desk.
6. Stand up.
7. Run in place.
8. Freeze and be completely still.
9. Put both hands over your eyes.
10. Uncover your eyes.
11. Take one step forward.
12. Take two steps backwards.
13. Pat your head three times.
14. Pat your stomach four times.
15. Tap with your right foot two times.
16. Tap with your left foot two times.
17. Sit down.
18. Repeat each word after the teacher:
    - "I"
    - "Can"
    - "Follow"
    - "Directions"

Teacher Directions *Verbal and Physical*

Walk Across the Capitals

Materials Needed: five copies of the letters below and on page 21; scissors

Directions: Make five copies of the letters below and on page 21. Be sure to make enough copies so you will have plenty of letters. Cut out the letters found in the space below and on page 22. Complete this activity in an area where with plenty of space.

Place the cutout letters on the floor. Notice not all letters in the alphabet are included because not all letters change form from lower case to capital. Tell the students you are going to play a game where the students must be able to recognize capital letters. Line students up at different capital letters. Tell the students they must cross to the other side of the room from where they start. They can only step on letters that are capital letters. They should step, not jump. If they accidentally step on a lowercase letter, they must go back to their beginning letter and start again. Their feet can be off the edges of the letters.

Hint: Depending on the size of the classroom, you might want to divide the class in half and let the students play in smaller groups or make extra play areas and divide the students into smaller groups while everyone plays at the same time.

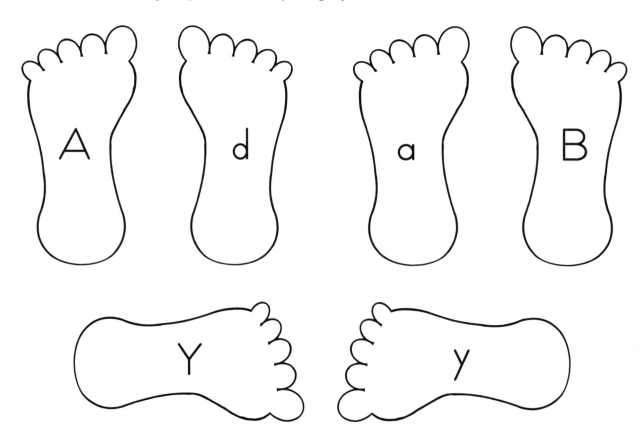

Teacher Directions   *Verbal and Physical*

Walk
Across the Capitals (cont.)

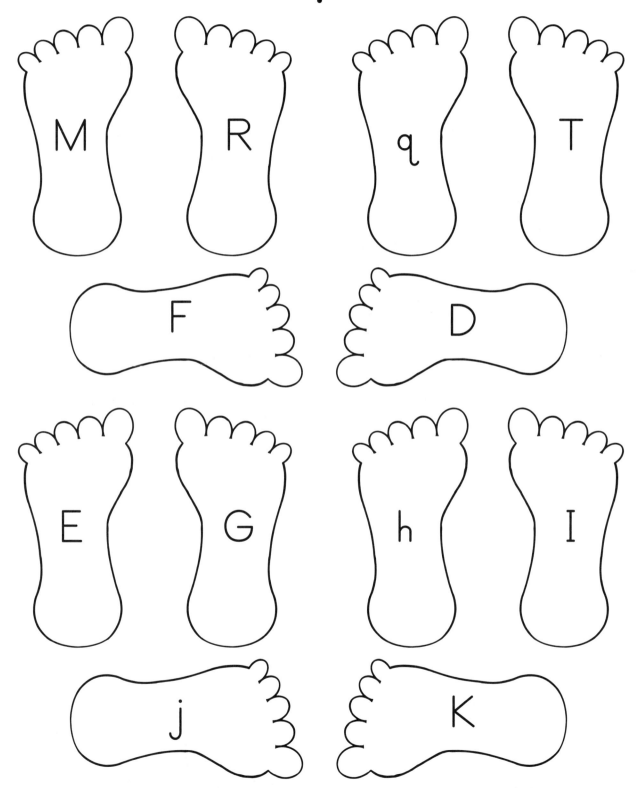

Teacher Directions *Verbal and Physical*

Doing the Duct Walk

Materials Needed: one roll of duct tape (any color)

Directions: Tell students that this is an activity to help them listen and follow directions.

Use the duct tape to make a square on the floor that is large enough for all of the students in the class to sit around the edges. Hint: If space is a problem, create two smaller squares rather than one large square. Both squares will follow the same directions.

Have students sit around the edges of the square. You, the teacher, will be the first leader. The leader will stand in the middle of the square. The leader decides which student will be chosen. The leader will tap a student on the shoulder, and that student will stand up but will not go to the center of the square. The leader will stay in the center of the square and will use the list of actions below to give a direction to the student who is standing outside the square.

Once the student is given a direction, he will hop, skip, run, etc., around the square until he makes it back to his original place. Then he will go to the center of the square and take the teacher's place. The teacher will move outside the square to monitor the game; however, after this turn, when the student in the center of the square is finished, he will sit back down in the place the new leader will vacate. Now the new leader in the center of the square will choose a new student to go next, and play will continue until all students have had a turn. Actions from the list can be repeated. Only choose actions you feel your students can safely complete.

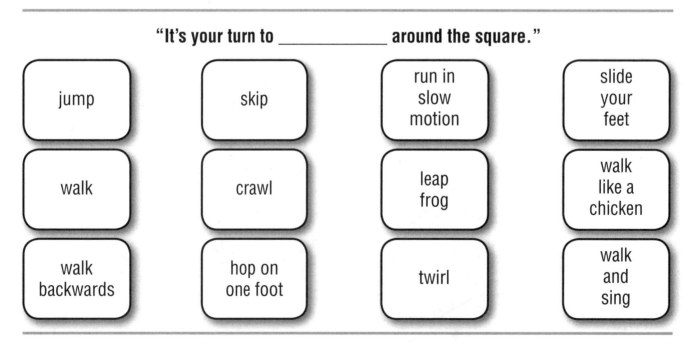

"It's your turn to _____ around the square."

jump	skip	run in slow motion	slide your feet
walk	crawl	leap frog	walk like a chicken
walk backwards	hop on one foot	twirl	walk and sing

Name: _____   Writing and Written

Find the One That Is Different

Directions: Color the pictures that are all the same in each row.

1.

2.

3.

4.

5.

Name: _____   Writing and Written

What's Before, Between, and After?

Part 1 Directions: Write the letter that comes before the letters in the alphabet.

1. ___ , e , f
2. ___ , b , c
3. ___ , y , z
4. ___ , m , n

Part 2 Directions: Write the letter that comes between the letters in the alphabet.

5. h , ___ , j
6. o , ___ , q
7. u , ___ , w
8. a , ___ , c

Part 3 Directions: Write the letter that comes after the letters in the alphabet.

9. h , i , ___
10. m , n , ___
11. r , s , ___
12. x , y , ___

Part 4 Directions: Write the number that comes before *and* the number that comes after.

13. ___ , 8 , ___
14. ___ , 4 , ___

#8710 Following Directions   24   ©Teacher Created Resources

Name: _____ *Writing and Written*

One Really Hot Dot-to-Dot

Materials Needed: crayons

Directions: Connect the dots to find out what is hot! Start with #1. Color the picture.

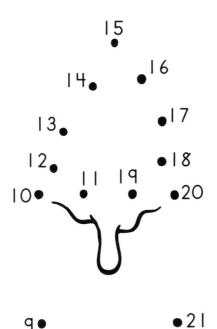

Name: _____   ***Writing and Written***

An Alphabet Connect the Dots

Materials Needed: crayons

Directions: Connect the dots. Start with the letter "A." Color the picture.

#8710 Following Directions   26   ©Teacher Created Resources

Name: _____ *Writing and Written*

Have Some First-Letter Fun

Directions: Look at each picture. Write the first letter of each word. Use lowercase.

1.

2.

3.

4.

5.

Name: _____   Writing and Written

Should You Circle or Underline?

Directions: Circle each letter. Underline each number. The first one has been done for you.

---

        2   6   K

S   t   y

3   5   F   f

X   P   10

7   Z   W   n

J   Y   4

R   s   r   N

8   C   d

Name: _____

Writing and Written

Red Triangles and Blue Squares

Materials Needed: three crayons (one red, one blue, one yellow)

Directions: Follow the rules to color each shape.

- Color the triangles **red**.
- Color the squares **blue**.
- Color the circles **yellow**.

©Teacher Created Resources — #8710 Following Directions

Name: _____   *Writing and Written*

How Many Do You See?

Directions: Write numbers to finish the story. Use the picture for clues.

The Park

There is _____ squirrel under the tree. The squirrel has _____ nuts. There are _____ birds sitting on the fence. There are _____ flowers growing on the grass.

Something Extra: On the back of the page, draw and color a picture of you at the park.

Name: _____   *Writing and Written*

Shape Names and Numbers

Directions: Count the shapes. Write the number. Write the word for the number.

	Number	Name
1. △△△△△	----------	--------------------

	Number	Name
2. ♡♡	----------	--------------------

	Number	Name
3. ○○○○○○○	----------	--------------------

	Number	Name
4. ☐☐☐☐☐☐☐☐☐	----------	--------------------

	Number	Name
5. ◇◇◇◇	----------	--------------------

	Number	Name
6. ☆☆☆☆☆☆☆	----------	--------------------

©Teacher Created Resources   #8710 Following Directions

Name: _____   *Writing and Written*

Same Beginning Sound

Directions: Say the names of the pictures in each square. Circle and color the pictures that **begin** with the same sound.

1.

2.

3.

4.

5.

6.

#8710 Following Directions   32   ©*Teacher Created Resources*

Name: _____ **Writing and Written**

Ending With the Same Sound

Directions: Say the names of the pictures in each square. Circle and color the pictures that have the same **ending** sound.

1.

2.

3.

4.

5.

6.

©Teacher Created Resources 33 #8710 Following Directions

Name: _____   *Writing and Written*

Writing Lowercase Letters

Directions: Look at the capital letter. Write the lowercase letter.

Example:

1. S ___
2. A ___
3. B ___
4. M ___
5. T ___
6. Z ___
7. B ___
8. I ___
9. F ___
10. D ___
11. W ___
12. L ___
13. C ___
14. E ___

Name: _____   Writing and Written

Match the Letter to the Sound

Directions: Say the letter. Match the letter to the picture that has the same beginning sound. Draw a line from the letter to the picture.

1. **B**

   plane   strawberry   butterfly

2. **M**

   monkey   apple   chair

3. **Z**

   star   zebra   yo-yo

4. **C**

   glasses   fish   carrot

5. **P**

   penguin   snowflake   gloves

6. **G**

   kite   giraffe   sun

©Teacher Created Resources   #8710 Following Directions

Name: _____

Writing and Written

Trace Before You Write

Directions: Trace each number. Write each number twice.

0 0 0

1 1 1

2 2 2

3 3 3

4 4 4

5 5 5

6 6 6

7 7 7

Name: _____ *Writing and Written*

More Trace Before You Write

Directions: Trace each number. Write each number twice.

8   8   8

9   9   9

10   10   10

11   11   11

12   12   12

13   13   13

14   14   14

15   15   15

©Teacher Created Resources #8710 Following Directions

Name: _____   *Writing and Written*

Color By the Numbers

Materials Needed: crayons

Directions: Use the numbers to help color the picture.

- Color each **1** green.
- Color each **2** blue.
- Color each **3** black.
- Color each **4** yellow.
- Color each **5** brown.
- Color each **6** red.

#8710 Following Directions ©Teacher Created Resources

Name: _____

Writing and Written

Trace All of the Shapes

Materials Needed: crayons

Directions: Read each direction. Trace the shapes.

1. Trace the shapes with a red crayon.

  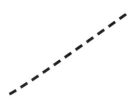

2. Trace the shapes with a blue crayon.

  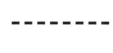

3. Trace the shapes with a green crayon.

4. Trace the shapes with a purple crayon.

5. Trace the shapes with a black crayon.

Name: _____   Writing and Written

Writing and Drawing Nouns

Directions: Write a noun that starts with each beginning sound. Draw and color a picture of each word.

1.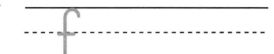

2.

3.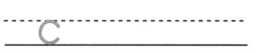

4.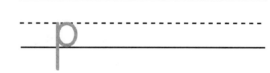

5.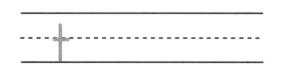

6.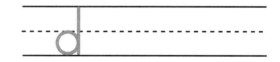

#8710 Following Directions · 40 · ©Teacher Created Resources

Teacher Directions — *Writing and Written*

Listen and Then Write

Materials Needed: paper (one piece per student); pencils (one per students)

Directions: Tell the students that you will be doing an activity where they must listen and then write. Read each direction slowly and clearly. Allow time for the students to write. Between directions, walk around the room to see if anyone needs help and that all students are on task.

Listen and Write List

1. Write a capital letter **A**.
2. Write the number **0**.
3. Draw a horizontal line.
4. Draw a triangle.
5. Write a lowercase **e**.
6. Draw a circle.
7. Write the number **11**.
8. Draw two squares.
9. Draw a heart.
10. Write a capital letter **T**.
11. Draw a tall rectangle.
12. Write the number **7** three times.
13. Draw a circle with a line through it.
14. Draw a triangle sitting on top of a square.
15. Write an uppercase **G** and a lowercase **g**.

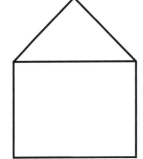

©Teacher Created Resources — #8710 Following Directions

Teacher Directions   Partners and Groups

How Words Begin and End

Materials Needed: pencils (one per student); scissors; one copy each of pages 43 and 44; copies of page 45 (one per student)

Directions:

- Make one copy each of page 43 and page 44. Cut out the cards. Divide the students into groups of four or five.

- Make copies of page 45 and distribute one to each student.

- Cut out the cards and stack them into a deck. Have each group choose four cards from the deck. It does not matter if all of the cards are used.

- Tell each group to read the letters or letter groups out loud. Decide what sound the letters or letter groups make. Give each group 5–7 minutes to write as many words as they can that begin or end with the letters or letter groups they have chosen from the four cards. Each child should write his or her answers on his or her own answer sheet (page 45). Once the time is up, the groups should rotate their four cards in a clockwise direction. The activity will continue until all groups have had a chance to complete all of the cards that were passed out.

- At the end of the time, collect the cards and write the letters or letter groups that were used on the board. Write the letters or letter groups in columns. Next, choose students from each group to come to the board and write a word for each column. Tell students to only add a word to the list on the board if it has not already been written on the board. Students can bring their own lists up to the board or a list from any member in their group. You should call several students to the board. Once several students have gone, be sure to ask the students if they have any other words on their sheets that were not included on the board. Add these to the list on the board.

- Read each word out loud and have the class repeat the word. Talk about the definition of any unusual words. Stress the sounds each letter or letter groups make.

Hint: New cards can be made and used for the activity if a teacher needs to specifically teach only certain letter sounds.

#8710 Following Directions   42   ©Teacher Created Resources

Teacher Directions   *Partners and Groups*

How Words Begin and End (cont.)

Directions: Cut out the following cards to use with the activity on page 42.

sc	g	er
ly	e	ing
ug	un	at
c	y	ap

Teacher Directions   *Partners and Groups*

How Words Begin and End (cont.)

Directions: Cut out the following cards to use with the activity on page 42.

cl	sh	an
d	b	p
g	qu	x
w	m	sk

Name: _____   *Partners and Groups*

How Words Begin and End (cont.)

Directions: Look at each set of cards. Say the letter or sound.

- In the **first** column, write the **letter or sound**.
- In the **second** column, write words that **begin with the same letter or sound**.
- In the **third** column, write words that **end with the same letter or sound**.

Use the back of the page if you need more space.

Letter or Sound	Same Beginning Sound	Same Ending Sound
1.		
2.		
3.		
4.		
5.		
6.		
7.		
8.		

©Teacher Created Resources

Teacher Directions *Partners and Groups*

Getting to Know Each Other

Materials Needed: paper (one piece per student); pencils (one per student)

Directions: Tell the students that this is an activity where they must listen carefully to each direction. Tell them they will have a chance to get to know their classmates better as they complete the activity. Students will need to number their papers 1–10.

Use the list of statements below to help the students complete the activity. Tell students you will read a statement. The students are to listen to the statement and then try to find someone in the room who matches each statement. The students only need to find one student who matches each statement. The student who is found that matches the statement must write his or her first name on the other student's paper. Students then wait for the next statement. If no students can be found that fit the description, the teacher can move on to the next one.

List of Statements

1. This person's favorite food is pizza.
2. This person has a pet cat.
3. This person has brown eyes.
4. This person is wearing tennis shoes.
5. This person is wearing a ring.
6. This person is wearing the color red.
7. This person has a sister.
8. This person has four or more letters in his or her first name.
9. This person has a lunchbox at school.
10. This person has blonde hair.

Answer Key

Page 12 — Following Directions with Ordinal Numbers

2. red circle is first
3. green circle is third
4. orange circle is sixth
5. blue circle is second
6. purple circle is fifth
7. yellow circle is fourth
8. red is first
   blue is second
   green is third
   yellow is fourth
   purple is fifth
   orange is sixth

Page 14 — Stop! That's Not Correct

List #1: 1, 2, 3, 4, 5, 6, 7, 8, 9, 10
List #2: Sunday, Monday, Tuesday, Wednesday, Thursday, Friday, Saturday
List #3: 21, 22, 23, 24, 25, 26, 27
List #4: January, February, March, April, May, June
List #5: A, B, C, D, E, F, G, H, I
List #6: 10, 9, 8, 7, 6, 5, 4, 3, 2, 1
List #7: July, August, September, October, November, December
List #8: Q, R, S, T, U, V
List #9: 11, 12, 13, 14, 15, 16, 17, 18, 19, 20
List #10: ant, bear, cat, dog, elephant, fish, giraffe

Page 23 — Find the One That Is Different

1. Dogs 2, 3, and 4 should be circled.
2. Trees 1, 2, and 4 should be circled.
3. Homes 1, 2, and 3 should be circled.
4. Pictures 1, 3, and 4 should be circled.
5. Cakes 1, 2, and 3 should be circled.

Page 24 — What's Before, Between, and After?

1. d
2. a
3. x
4. l
5. i
6. p
7. v
8. b
9. j
10. o
11. t
12. z
13. 7, 9
14. 3, 5

Page 25 — One Really Hot Dot-to-Dot

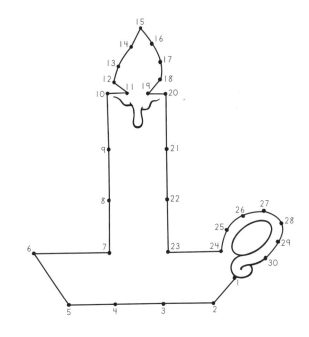

Page 26 — An Alphabet Connect the Dots

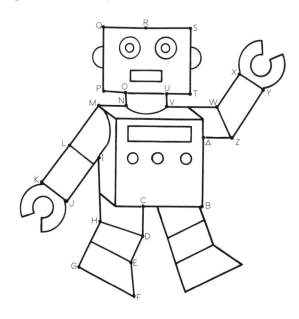

Answer Key (cont.)

Page 27 — Have Some First-Letter Fun
1. o, p, b
2. c, t, g
3. f, h, s
4. a, k, d
5. u, e, y

Page 28 — Should You Circle or Underline?
Circle:
M, K, S, t, y, F, f, X, P, Z, W, n, J, Y, R, s, r, N, C, d
Underline:
2, 6, 3, 5, 10, 7, 4, 8

Page 30 — How Many Do You See?
The Park
There is one (1) one squirrel under the tree. The squirrel has three (3) nuts.
There are two (2) birds sitting on the fence.
There are five (5) flowers growing on the grass.

Page 31 — Shape Names and Numbers
1. 5, five
2. 2, two
3. 7, seven
4. 9, nine
5. 4, four
6. 8, eight

Page 32 — Same Beginning Sound
1. balloon, basketball, broom
2. pencil, pie, pirate
3. cupcake, cat, cow
4. tree, tiger, tire
5. kite, king, kangaroo
6. dog, deer, diamond

Page 33 — Ending With the Same Sound
1. dress, shoes, bus
2. clock, rock, duck
3. pig, dog, frog
4. wheel, school, bowl
5. box, fox, ax
6. bell, snail, seal

Page 34 — Writing Lowercase Letters
1. s
2. a
3. b
4. m
5. t
6. z
7. b
8. i
9. f
10. d
11. w
12. l
13. c
14. e

Page 35 — Match the Letter to the Sound
1. butterfly
2. monkey
3. zebra
4. carrot
5. penguin
6. giraffe

Page 41 — Listen and Then Write
1. A
2. 0
3. ——
4. △
5. e
6. ○
7. 11
8. □□
9. ♡
10. T
11. □
12. 777
13. ⊖
14. ⌂
15. Gg